photo by Dickie Anderson.
ight 2003.

over:
0-9741042-1-3
dition
rinting

of Congress Control Number: 2003108307

er: Published by:
Maker   Market Maker
arsh Lakes Drive   (904) 261-2425
dina Beach, FL 32034
m@bellsouth.net
61-2425
ickieAnderson.com
m@bellsouth.net

MW01595521

FROM THE POF

Share Life's Unexpected

by Dickie Anderson

FRO
Dick
in an
recor
used

Cover
Copy

Hard
ISBN
First
First

Libra

To or
Marke
115 N
Ferna
dickie
(904)
www.
dickie

Capturing the simple, joy-filled experiences of everyday living, Anderson's words emphasize what is, and is not, important in life's brief journey. It is one of those rare books that you can pick up, turn to any page, and find yourself there.

Those who loved the first "Porch" book will be enthralled with the second collection of heartwarming stories that capture the unexpected joys in our everyday lives.

Praise for Dickie's Writing

"Her humorous essays celebrate nature, from as simple as a walk through the home garden to discovering the wonders of Cumberland Island. Anderson brings more smiles with the trials of modern living with dealing with technology and computer viruses. She plays homage to her community with her essays."

~Joyce Dixon - *Southern Scribe*

Dickie Anderson has a talent for honing in on life's little things, as she shares her interesting observations about local life and her personal experiences. With words, she masterfully paints a portrait of living in a charming seaside community, that she fondly calls "Mayberry By The Sea." Reading this collection of short stories, now published under hard cover, will offer the reader an inner glimpse into this small-town community.

~Barbara Lawson– *Amelia Island Lifestyle*

A special thank you to Shelly,
my ever patient and supportive husband;
my beloved trio of boys and their "girls";
Susan Gallion, a very special talent, friend and editor;
a dynamic duo, Gill and Barbara Johnston
and my much loved "island women"
who light up my life each and every day.

IN MEMORY OF MY FATHER FRANKLIN A. DICK

CONTENTS

FALL

WINTER

Introduction

Well, back to the porch. After the success of the first FROM THE PORCH book, it became clear a second needed to follow. You will find columns that have been selected from the weekly columns that appear in the Wednesday *Florida Times-UnionNassau Neighbors* publication, with a few surprises.

Reprinted by permission of:
Nassau Neighbors, *The Florida Times-Union*, Amelia Island, Florida.
Read current or archived *From the Porch* columns online:

WWW. JACKSONVILLE.COM

SPRING

Hole in One

How many times have we watched a nervous, skinny guy go out on a football field or to the centerline of a basketball court and attempt to make an impossible shot? We all love to watch and dream about beating the odds—the chance to win thousands of dollars, a trip to somewhere exotic, or maybe even a car.

Haven't we all taken a chance? Trying to knock bottles down with a baseball or purchasing a chance to win a prize? We rationalize that it's for a worthy cause, and usually it is. Yes, we even buy lottery tickets, knowing that we might as well burn the money. We pay out our dollars and are pleased that we can benefit the high school cheerleaders, a church youth group or another equally worthy cause. But who expects to actually win?

Our community holds lots of golf tournaments. It is a popular way to raise money for the many non-profits that depend on generosity and enthusiasm for their endeavors. For many it is a chance to get away from the daily office grind, take a nice, long walk through a beautiful, tree-lined golf course, maybe drink a little beer and conduct a little business.

One sunny Friday not too long ago a group gathered at a local golf club to raise money for the rapidly expanding island YMCA. Bankers, car dealers, realtors, fast food entrepreneurs and many more turned out. My husband, a life-long golfer, grumbled all week about no time for practice, adding that he really shouldn't take the time to play. But he badly needed a day with the boys and a little ball slamming therapy, so I pushed him out the door.

Late in the afternoon, the day of the tournament, the phone rang and I turned from my computer to answer it. It was my golfer, but there was something odd about this call. It was a noisy one, with lots of other voices in the background, and my husband couldn't contain his excitement as he hollered, "Guess what?!"

"You won the tournament?" I asked hopefully.

"No," he exclaimed, "I got a hole in one and WON A CAR!!" After asking him three times if he really got a hole in one and really won a car, I finally believed him. A dream come true for any golfer—a hole in one, and on top of that, a new car!

As my husband tells the tale, he approached a challenging par 3 hole and noticed the prize car parked next to the green. Everyone admired the car and joked about what little chance they had to gain that elusive hole in one.

My hero stepped up, addressed the ball, did his little wiggle and hit the golf ball straight at the hole. It hit the front of the green and continued to move toward the hole, and then… disappeared. One of his partners yelled at the young lady, the official "watcher," who was standing nearby. She was dumbfounded and not sure what to do. She had been told not to worry—no one *ever* gets a hole in one. The chance of getting a hole in one is no better than winning the lottery.

As they say, the crowd went wild. Golfers from nearby holes rushed over to confirm the hole in one. One especially interested party was the car dealer, who had donated the car and was playing in the foursome ahead. He, too, was a bit unsure of what to do and was probably secretly praying that the insurance that covers such a long shot was in place.

Anticipating the homecoming of "Ace Anderson," champagne was put on ice and a big sign and balloon were attached to our mailbox. The magic of the moment lasted for days as the hero would stop, smile and remark on how unbelievable his experience had been.

Still know as "the guy who got a hole in one and won a car", my resident celebrity still enjoys recalling his masterful hole in one.

Car Talk

Cars are guy things, at least at our house. I cannot tell one from another—with a few exceptions: I can pick out a Jaguar or a Mercedes and a convertible *anything*. Raised in a classically chauvinistic family, there has never been a question in my mind about who takes care of the family cars. These things and more are clearly in "his" column: dead batteries, oil changes, bad tires, and tune-ups. I am less chauvinistic and more willing to "share" when it comes to laundry and kitchen time.

Deciding on family transportation can be an interesting negotiation. How does one decide what kind of vehicle to buy? When I was growing up people were loyal to one brand of automobile. You were Ford people or you were Chevy people, and so on—almost like belonging to a political party. Times have changed and you are more likely to hear people refer to cars by their model names: Cherokee, Blazer, Sebring, Tahoe, Suburban. It is interesting that some brand names have not only endured, but have taken on a life of their own. Some classic cars of the past exemplify the best and have even become descriptive words. Being a "Cadillac" or a "Mercedes" is a very good thing. Then there is the other extreme—a car that is a disaster and represents a bust. Many of us remember the dubious Edsel—a bad thing.

Renting cars allows us to try out different brands and models, which can be an adventure. In my former busy, ever-traveling life, I had the opportunity to rent a lot of cars.

The cars became generic to me and I felt like just another white dot on the highway. On one particular trip I parked my shiny, white car in a multi-level garage and went to my conference. When I returned to the garage all I could see was row after row of shiny, white cars. What would distinguish mine from the herd? Thank God for my Nordstrom's bag on the back window ledge.

Rental cars might also help us decide what not to buy in the future. Why, oh, why do car designers find new and frustrating places to put basic controls like the ignition or air handling systems? Many of us experience being frozen in the driver's seat, or wondering how to turn on the heat or the defroster, or simply lock or unlock the doors.

On yet another business trip I experienced near panic. With moments to spare, I stopped to fill the tank of my rental car before turning it in at the airport. I pulled up to a self-serve gas station (having recently become empowered to pump my own gas), and jumped out of the car. Walking around the car several times I could find no visible gas tank. Compromising my newfound gas station confidence, I asked a man for help. The attendant smiled that smile a man smiles when a woman has a car issue. He sauntered confidently to the back end of the car where he flipped up the license plate to reveal a cleverly hidden gas tank.

What about the cars at our house? We have our Blazer or "the truck" as we call it—*his* car. And my car? A convertible, of course.

Car Trips

As much as we love our hometown, we all like to escape occasionally. We often travel by automobile and appreciate the convenience it affords us. As we travel by car we sometimes talk about car trips remembered from our own childhoods and the childhoods of our kids. Long trips and small spaces challenge any family and even old married couples.

More often than not our longer car trips are to visit our children who have settled in various parts of the country. Traveling by car allows the luxury of taking along whatever you want. And we do. We take several of the books in progress or waiting to be read, yellow pads to make notes, books on tape from the library, and I usually have a knitting project or two. Often our trips away from home are no more than a couple of days, but we have enough material for weeks or maybe years in some remote outback.

Food and drink are problematic. Often we do not get out of our county without stopping for a cup of coffee or something to eat. We are forever spilling coffee and forever vowing never again—no coffee in the car. The ban lasts no more than overnight, as we grasp with iron-like fists our morning coffee, which travels with us to our first destination. Yes, we are guilty of the fast food thing too, regretting it before we finish our greasy drive-through meal.

We remember those trips *with* children and *as* children. As a child I remember cross-country trips that seemed to take years. We tried to make long days short. We played car games: the license plate game, "grandmother's trunk," and pad and pencil games like "battleship" and "hangman." There are memories of kids who got carsick, things left behind and even memories of keys locked in cars early in the morning in the middle of "Nowhere," Pennsylvania.

A fond memory from my childhood trips were our family sing-a-longs—often gems from classic Broadway shows. Hearing those songs today still transports me to the backseat of a Ford Fairlane and the long drive from Chicago to Baltimore that we made each Thanksgiving.

Other memories involved backseat territorial rights. "She's on my side…" or "he pushed me" coming from a frustrated child in the backseat. Sometimes the combatants knew they had gone too far and incurred the wrath of the driver. Not good. Deadly quiet. If the car slowed and pulled over to the side of the road you knew you were in serious trouble.

Windshield time is good time. We do catch up on things, complete sentences and listen a little more closely as our mates share their thoughts and plans. I am not the best of companions, as I tend to go to sleep within minutes of embarking on a long car trip—the quiet, the soft humming of the engine and the motion simply lull me to sleep. Some get carsick, I get *car-sleep*. My companion says he misses my company… hmmm.

Packing – The Game

Packing for a trip is a challenge. It doesn't matter whether your destination is Cleveland or Paris. In addition to the usual challenges of how much is too much, airport security regulations have changed the rules. Be sure the nail file, Swiss Army knife, scissors and quintessential wine bottle opener are safely stowed in your check-through luggage. And don't forget the oft-repeated rule of the road: Carry the necessities of life in case you are separated from your checked luggage.

The stakes of the game go up when travel takes you abroad. One spring, as we planned a trip to France, we decided to check with our more experienced global traveling friends. My husband's eyes got big as we listened to tales of lost luggage and bands of gypsies preying on travel weary tourists. We were reminded again and again the importance of having your passport and money close at hand and not easily accessible to clever gangs of thieves. We briefly considered using man's best friend, duct tape, and taping our essentials to our bodies.

Our guest room bed became the "game board". As our travel date grew closer, we began to pile up various items that we might need or were afraid we would forget. What you take and how you pack is determined by your planned activities, climate and length of time you will be gone. Each square inch of your baggage is precious and must be used effectively.

Our game rules were further defined by our itinerary and mode of travel. We were to join a group in Southern France and bicycle for two weeks through the rolling hills of Provence. We were limited to one duffel bag and one backpack each. Once we met our group in France, our baggage would be transported from spot to spot; the challenge was to get to our group with two duffel bags, two backpacks, our passports and money in tact.

First priority? Selecting the appropriate clothing for our daily bicycling. We shopped state-of-the-art catalogs and local bicycle shops to find the specialty wear suitable for bicycling. We learned about every synthetic fiber known to man that washes and dries quickly, while keeping you either warm or cool, depending on the weather. In the end, we ordered smart, stopping just short of pith helmets and the photographer's vest with its endless pockets. A small part of the duffel was allotted for after-hours clothing—something nice to wear to dinner. I said a thank-you prayer to the traveling woman's savior: wrinkle-free, slinky, synthetic fabric clothing that can be stuffed into small spaces.

I discovered packing cubes. A delightful invention—different sized, cunningly designed, zippered bags that hold specific categories of clothing, underwear, tops and bottoms. I smugly tucked each "cube" into my duffel, confidant that I would stay organized as we traveled. Funny, on the way home every cube was filled with the same thing—dirty clothes.

Lists were made and the piles on the guest room bed grew. The piles included the prerequisite black "sausage pants," neon windbreakers, waterproof jackets, layers of Cool Max, and, of course, my favorite modern invention—fleece. As the day of departure grew closer, the piles grew smaller. Items had to be eliminated for the final cut.

Other basics included bandanas (you can never have too many), a medical kit, Neosporin, aspirin, anti-diarrhea medicine, earplugs, sewing kit, blister remedies and sun block. We remembered converters for the hairdryer and batteries for the camera.

Then came the day of reckoning. Our duffels were packed tight as drums and our backpacks overflowed with the basics. For us, the basics always include water and a couple of good books to read on the endless plane trip across the ocean. We looked at each other, smiled like two youngsters leaving for summer camp, and headed out the door.

Hours later on a plane high over the Atlantic Ocean we did what all travelers do. We tried to remember what we had packed and what we might have forgotten.

France On A Bicycle

Folks often ask us about our bicycle trip to Southern France. One aspect of the trip that seems to attract the most curiosity is the fact that we did it on bicycles. Anyone can go to Provence and eat wonderful food and drink delicious wine. But on a bicycle? We still get looks of concern regarding our sanity and stunned amazement that we survived.

Daily trips ranged from twenty to forty miles. The terrain was described as "moderately rolling" in the materials we received prior to departure. While "rolling" to an experienced rider may seem like a gentle hill, our training rides on Florida's flat roads did not prepare us for France's hills which seemed more like alps to us. Whenever necessary we swallowed our pride and walked our bikes over the tougher hills. We could always rationalize—walking is good exercise too, especially when you're pushing a bike along with you.

Our two delightful tour leaders, Pasquale and Sophie, made the trip through Provence enjoyable and safe. On the first evening our group of eighteen met to share wine and sample some local delicacies. Pasquale, elfin and with a twinkle in his eye, and Sophie, a Peter Pan look-alike, reviewed the next week and half we would share. We were given basic tips about the drivers and roads in France. Pasquale winked as he said, "Ah, yes, it is true the French drivers they drive very, very fast, but they drive very good." Unlike the great behemoths that crowd our roads in the United States, cars in France are small—not much bigger than the bumper cars one sees in carnivals. Don't let their size fool you, though. They can move very fast. We were encouraged to attend a flat tire class the next morning.

Some friends have asked us about the bicycles we rode. Experienced bicycle riders know that the quality and fit of the bike does make a difference. We rode "hybrids" supplied by our tour company. A hybrid is a combination of a road touring bike and a mountain bike. Each of us had a bike suited to our height and weight.

They supplied us with helmets, tire repair kits, and square, black boxes that attached to our handlebars for holding daily essentials. My essentials included snacks, water, bandanas and my digital camera. We were cautioned to take the detachable bags with us when we stopped to eat, sightsee or shop;. we carried them like large, awkward purses. We would lock several bikes together creating a cluster that made them impossible to steal and sometimes nearly impossible to separate.

My spouse and I had carefully planned ahead for our travel and biking gear. The bright neon colors that bicycle riders sport? They have a purpose. Visibility is key—you want those drivers, speeding through the countryside in their tiny French cars, to see you. We were hard to miss in our glowing greens, pinks and blues of quick drying, sweat wicking, wonder fabrics.

Our luggage would go ahead of us each day. Our support van circled the route, with one guide in the vehicle and the other riding with the group. We knew help was never long in coming. When you set eighteen Americans off on bicycles in the wilds of Southern France there are bound to be adventures. We had our share—flat tires; battles with the fabled Mistral winds; and more than a few unexpected, delightful detours (otherwise known as getting lost).

Each morning would start with a traditional French breakfast of large, fluffy croissants; fresh fruit; dark, chewy, local sausages; and fragrant, rich coffee. As we finished our morning feast, Pasquale and Sophie would review the day ahead. This routine took on the character of a military campaign—detailed maps, warnings regarding bad roads, difficult turns to find and perhaps a hill or two. Then we were off to our rooms, into our spandex and quickly on the road by nine o'clock. We did not ride together in a line with a leader at front and back. We fell into smaller groups, setting our own pace.

Many picture the colorful Tour de France with its dashing riders bicycling at breakneck speed in neat lines through the patchwork of quaint countryside. Think again: try picturing the tortoise, not the hare, and a pace that moves forward, just not at lightning speed. Yes, it is work and sometimes you question your own sanity and likelihood of survival. But traveling by bicycle beats spilling out of a monster bus with 75 other people, more than half of whom you don't particularly like; getting in line for "les toilettes;" and interminable waits at restaurants that are unprepared for a large group.

Instead, each day as the lunch hour neared, we would find yet another impossibly picturesque town and ride slowly through the cobblestone streets.

Our café radar would lead us to a cluster of brightly colored umbrellas—a new, delightful spot to have lunch and maybe a petit vin rouge.

To see a country with the wind at your back and quiet wheels turning beneath you is to experience its very essence. As we passed vineyard after vineyard, and fields planted with vegetables and fruits of all kinds, people would wave and smile, giving us a cheerful "bonjour." We saw carpets of bright red poppies in bloom, stopped and ate cherries right off the trees, and smelled the earthy perfume of lush countryside.

It was strenuous, but no one judged you if you jumped on the van or took a time-out. And we knew that at the end of the day there would be hot water and cold wine. Would we do it again? In a heartbeat.

French Cooking

Back from a wonderful trip to France, my husband and I found ourselves full of enthusiasm gained from an unforgettable cooking class we had taken on a sunny May morning. We shared fragrant memories of that kitchen in southern France.

Determined to capture the simplicity and essence of our meals in Provence, we decided to invest in what we perceived were the essentials. With years of feeding a young family far behind us, we have fallen into habits that have reduced our efforts in the kitchen to pushing buttons on the microwave or opting for the menu choice of "eating out." To be fair, I must add that my commendable husband truly enjoys shopping for a fresh piece of fish or meat and preparing it on the grill with simple accompaniments, which might include just-picked local tomatoes and fruit.

Our culinary adventure began in a simple kitchen in a small hotel near St. Rèmy in Provençe, France. Our hotel's energetic and talented chef, Hérvé Gely, provided a hands-on demonstration as he prepared several typical Provençal dishes, including ratatouille and tapenade. The simplicity of the kitchen, the equipment and the attention to detail impressed us all, but especially my resident fledgling chef.

More or less settled back at home, we set out to find the correct equipment, vowing to rid our cupboards of the clutter and utensils never used or hopelessly redundant. The first item on our list was *the* knife. Each exposure to gourmet cooking seems to begin with the essential and favorite knife. A set of knives to a good cook is a very personal thing. Hérvé used a basic favorite and minced and diced with what seemed like reckless abandon. His knife glistened as he rapidly chopped various vegetables. The rhythm and speed were hypnotizing as we all stood in wonder that his fingers remained intact.

Hérvé s short list of essentials included basic pans for sautéing, several qualities of olive oil, a constant and reliable heat source, and, always, the very freshest of herbs and vegetables. We spent several hours with Hérvé and marveled at his talent. We looked forward to the meal he would prepare for us that evening. We were rewarded. As we gathered for a glass of local wine before dinner, we looked down into a terraced garden behind the hotel. There was Hérvé, in full, bright, white chef regalia, cutting herbs, and picking strawberries and fresh vegetables for our evening meal.

Fast forward. Now fully recovered from jet lag and determined to eat better, we headed straight for the nursery where we purchased some basic fresh herbs. They had added such wonderful and subtle flavors to our meals in France. We bought basil, oregano and rosemary. The perfume of vibrant herbs filled the car as we continued on to the gourmet cooking supply shop. We found the essential knife and several other little tools that would surely enhance our cooking efforts.

Then... on to the kitchen and our first attempt. We had a grand time, sharing the kitchen and remembering Hérvé as we sliced, diced and sautéed. Our first masterpiece was a large dish of ratatouille—a wonderful medley of eggplant, zucchini, onion and red pepper (but no tomatoes per Hérvé's warning of *too mushy*). Our dogs, accustomed to more mundane kitchen droppings, were initially confused as bits of onion and eggplant hit the floor; but they soon became part of our French cuisine family time.

Enjoying our meal on the porch, we congratulated ourselves and planned our next cooking adventure in our currently very neat and well-equipped kitchen.

Slow Food

Think about how we eat. Few of us take time to savor the food we eat every day. Our meals are more about speed than enjoyment. Fast food restaurants dot every highway, luring passing drivers in for a quick fix. We all know the familiar signs and logos.

In a hurry, we turn into one of the many fast food restaurants lining our busy, local main street. We pull into the line like sheep in a chute. First stop is the posted menu and the wait for the little box to squawk at us. How silly we must look talking to a brightly colored sign. Between the antiquated mechanical device that asks for the order, and the person at the other end taking orders, communication is challenging at best.

Desperately we repeat our order until we come to some sort of understanding and are instructed to move to the first window. We move slowly forward wondering if the voice meant the first window we come to or the next window. A smiling face looks out of the first window, ready to take the money. We dig for our money and hope that no coins are dropped as the transfer is made. We proceed to the next window and pick up our bag chock full of quick food.

We are handed a crinkly bag of bags, plus assorted straws, seasonings and sauces. Pulling away, an impatient hand explores the bag searching for

French fries. There is something about fast food French fries. There is nothing quite like them—fast food candy. Nibbling on the French fries, next we find the burger. We are now balancing a cold drink, hopefully secured in a drink holder of the correct size, with napkins in our lap, French fries close at hand, and a burger oozing with special sauce.

This is the critical period—proceed along your way determined to mind the traffic while eating and not spilling. There is a certain level of guilt as we consume the certifiably unhealthy fare, but it is easy to rationalize that one is saving time and money.

My family members are fast eaters. You would think eating was an Olympic competition—sparks fly as knives and forks hit the plate. We often look up from a meal, clean plates in front of us, to see that others have barely begun. Whoops. Forget about smelling the roses or savoring a gourmet meal.

We need to savor the moment and the art of lingering. Traveling in other countries, almost any other country, one finds that people take time to eat their meals. These people know how to eat. Meals are more than eating—they are time for friends and family. No rushing through a meal, no brown bags, and no eating at your desk. They savor their noonday meal and take no less than two hours—everything closes.

There is a lesson here. Maybe it is time for us to replace fast food with slow food.

Furry Friends

Many of my neighbors find themselves at war. The opponents may look like innocent Disney characters. But no, these furry little demons eat our gardens, attack our birdfeeders, and sneak into our garages and attics. Squirrels, moles and rabbits—they are intrepid and must be stopped.

Squirrels are in-your-face kind of pests. They wait as we hang our newest state-of-the-art birdfeeders and fill them with the seed *du jour*. Before long, the scouts, bobbing and weaving, circle and check out their newest challenge. The higher the price of the feeder the longer it may take for the squirrels to break the code, but they always do. For every human strategy and ingenious birdfeeder there is a smarter squirrel.

An on-going curse at our house is rabbits. They munch and chew anything but weeds. Why doesn't someone figure out how to breed rabbits that eat weeds? Touring the garden with morning coffee I note major damage to some new bedding plants. Where freshly planted flowers once had been all that remain are stubby little stems. I have confronted my husband, assuming that he had gone a bit crazy with the trimmer. His innocent look convinces me that the problem is not an over-exuberant weed whacker, but something far more insidious—rabbits.

Odd and varied strategies have been launched against the rabbits that continue to thrive in and around our backyard. Mothballs are placed around the most vulnerable plants. Special sprays and prescriptions were bought from local garden centers. The rabbits remain, undaunted and apparently multiplying. Even the self-manufactured spray created by my husband (don't ask) makes no difference. My backyard is ever dotted with small furry rabbits that slowly and surely go about their business of eating my plants. Our battle with the rabbits is a losing one.

Back to the squirrels. It has taken me half a lifetime to learn to "shift my paradigms" and to try looking at things in life in other ways. To turn negative things into positive things. Perhaps a shift is in order regarding squirrels.

Many of us love feeding birds and stocking our many feeders regularly. Perhaps we should, instead, feed the squirrels and consider the birds unwelcome visitors. There are, after all, people who *like* squirrels. Garden centers and nature stores offer special feeders that are designed for furry rather than feathered friends. Corn is a preferred diet, but as we feeders of birds know, sunflower seeds are filet mignon to feeder-raiding squirrels.

Squirrels *are* fun to watch—with their furling tails, twitching, small, bright eyes and tiny ears. Their antics, as they jump from tree to tree, are more entertaining than most television programs. Imagine looking out a window and rapping hard on the glass to scare birds off of your squirrel feeder.

It may be too tough to love squirrels at the expense of birds. Striking a balance may be a better option: equal opportunity feeders with seed for the birds and corn for the squirrels. Forget the rabbits—they seem to take care of themselves.

SUMMER

One-armed Writer

Surgery on my right hand created unexpected challenges to me. We have heard of one-armed bandits, but I became, at least temporarily, a one-armed writer. A nagging, painful arthritic condition led to outpatient surgery. A small bone was removed and a pad was put in its place made of recycled tendon from my wrist. I emerged from surgery flaunting a large, encumbering cast on my right hand and arm.

It occurred to me that it might be entertaining to create a more interesting explanation for my club-like right hand. Clearly a fabricated tale of fending off a rabid alligator in our backyard marsh, or being nipped by a shark while surfing, probably wouldn't sell. The mundane truth? Basically old age and arthritis.

Limited to the use of one hand, and my left one at that, I encounter new and different challenges. Attempts at handwriting look like badly drafted ransom notes. I could not sign my name. The checkbook was safe for a while—much to my husband's short-term glee. Little did he know... there are ways.

The day after surgery reality set in. I would have to do something about bathing and cleaning up. My husband stood ready as a reluctant bath attendant. With duct tape and plastic bags in hand I began what I assumed would be a lengthy and tedious process. The bathing part went smoothly. The warm, steamy water felt good to my traumatized body.

The challenges came as I tried to use the blow dryer and put some curl into my determinedly straight hair. I looked into the clouded mirror at my dripping hair. I called for assistance. A memory I will treasure is my husband trying to help me dry my hair and use my hot rollers. He stood behind me, good humored, but awkward; at one point we looked like one of those many-armed Indian idols. Job done, I struggled into clothing that would accommodate the club-like cast on my right hand.

My one-armedness severely compromised another habit—doing the daily crossword puzzle. Struggling to find archaic and/or clever definitions has long been a welcomed distraction in my daily routine. Bored? Try to do a crossword with your left hand (or right if you are left-handed). Not only do you try to think of words for rare coins, Greek Gods and tiny African countries, but also you have to read your own printing, which may include a backward "s" or "e". Double the pleasure? Double the frustration.

Yes, I got a lot of mileage out of the dramatic appearance of my wrapped appendage: increased portions of ice cream; no dishwashing duty; no vacuuming; and, delightful surprises, like a friend bringing chicken soup— yes, healing chicken soup. Another friend brought a beautiful plant. I chuckled when I read the tag stating that it was a "prayer plant." Hey, I'll take any help I can get.

Don't get ideas. The fifteen minutes of fame and attention are small compensation for being grounded. No tennis or yoga for this girl for three months. And typing using only one hand? It's a perverse intelligence test. So be extra nice to your right hand today—it deserves it!

Casserole Ladies

Thank you, my angels of the kitchen. A minor setback at our house created a phenomenon we are enjoyed thoroughly. It is a sweet mix of friendship and wonderful, portable Southern hospitality. Minor surgery on a hand left me more than a little compromised in the kitchen. Some might say that that has nothing to do with my bad paw, but anyway, thank heavens for the angels tapping on my door with wonderful things to eat.

My husband wondered how long and what type of illness or injury could trigger an additional flow of chicken soup, baked ham, berry pies and casseroles. Don't push, I said. The wonderful thing about the generosity of friends is knowing that it triggers in each of us the instinct to help the next one who has a setback.

My first experience with the wonderful and legendary casserole ladies happened many years ago as a young mother living in Durham, North Carolina. Coming home from the hospital after the birth of my third child, I found someone knocking on the door each afternoon with a complete meal for my young family. No one called, but every day for a week the doorbell would ring each afternoon and dinner would be delivered. Later when I became a full-fledged Casserole Lady, I learned that you simply take your day and ensure that you are not duplicating a meal, and that's that.

There is occasionally a dark side to this strong Southern tradition. It can get competitive. Southern women may have soft, gentle, musical voices and dress like ladies from decades past, but don't mess with their secret recipe for Aunt Sadie's Triple Pecan Orange Coffee Cake. Our church in those Durham days had Sunday night family suppers. The dessert table would look like the Pillsbury Bake-Off. And vegetable casseroles? No one does it better. I even learned to eat regional favorites like okra—one of those acquired tastes like fried green tomatoes.

The Casserole Ladies turn out for happy events, in times of illness, and also times of death. It is comforting to be able to do something when a family is dealing with so many comings and goings and decisions. Not having to worry about food is a great help. Comfort food is not only comforting to those who receive it, but it is also comforting to those who prepare it. It feels good to share and contribute.

A bittersweet memory stays with me. A friend, knowing she was dying of an evil, invasive cancer, reflected with her usual salty and ironic humor that she would be "barely cool" by the time the Casserole Ladies would come knocking on her husband's door with warm comfort foods. She saw the humor, and so did I months later after she lost her final battle and the Casserole Ladies came a knocking.

When the going gets tough the tough get cooking. What better way to do something for someone than to give the gift of not only something good to eat but the gift of not having to worry about a meal? So, thanks, each and every one—and if you didn't get your dish back let me know.

Cell Phone

Can't live with them and can't live without them. Like so many modern technologies which include the fax and email, cell phone use has spread faster than a bad virus. The cell phones have given us true instant communication, as evidenced by a phone ringing in the stall next to me in a recent stop to an airport ladies room. One really never knows where and when a phone may ring. When a cell phone rings in a crowded room everyone scrambles to find their phone, desperately digging in purses and pockets to stop the embarrassing ringing. The only thing missing is the Three Stooges.

We all have our own personal pet peeves that involve the use of cell phones and probably have equally impressive stories about how a cell phone has made a difference in a critical situation. I have been impressed both times I have been traveling in my car, passed a serious accident and called 911. The operator answering quickly got the needed information and confirmed that other calls had come in.

My pet peeves include the well-dressed businessmen in the airports doing business in loud self-important voices or striding through airports talking on their cell phones, oblivious to the traffic around them. In the midst of highly competitive tennis match, a ringing tennis bag is an unwelcome distraction. The impertinent ring of a cell phone spoils high drama in a darkened theater. The list goes on.

My original cell phone was purchased to have in the car in case of emergency. My husband, ever impatient that I never have my phone or if I do it isn't on, encouraged me to purchase one of the newer, easier to use phones and to carry it all the time. Fate stepped in as a cell phone rebate program literally paid for the spiffy little phone that fits neatly in a pocket of my purse. Gotta say I am enjoying the many conveniences it offers.

While visiting my oldest son and his wife in Washington DC the cell phone became a great communication tool. First, as I exited the plane I called my son who lives nearby and by the time I reached the curb he was waiting for me. With increased security at airports, those being dropped off or picked depend on instant communication. Cell phones allow travelers to make calls without tracking down a phone booth only to find it out of order or engaged. Memories of trying to find a phone in an airport to make a call include standing and staring at the person on the phone who will not look you in the eye, respond to your gestures and has clearly settled in for the long haul. Like bank lines, I always pick the wrong one.

On the same trip to Washington DC, we visited the Smithsonian museum in Washington. My son, his wife and I got separated. Not to worry a quick cell phone call and we met in the line at the I-Max movie theater and shared an afternoon in the Galapagos Islands.

Another convenience many of us appreciate is the caller ID feature. It helps to screen calls. Do you wonder that if no one answers that, perhaps, YOU have been screened? Guess what goes around comes around. Evidently telemarketers are now calling people on their cell phones. Talk about insult to injury. You get an unwanted solicitation call and you pay for it!

Galloping technology continues to take over our lives - cell phones, Palm Pilots, digital cameras, laptops, email. Think about it. We had never heard of any of these things ten years ago. Running hard to keep up with technology, I continue to be challenged by someone else who is a bit further down the futuristic highway. Catching up with a friend recently he looked down at his cell phone and said he had just gotten an email from his wife.

Email on my tiny little cell phone? What next?

Resort Casual

It always strikes me funny—the term "resort casual". Wondering what to wear to a social event in Florida? The quick and sometimes flip answer? "Resort Casual." Is there such a thing as "Resort Formal"? Who comes up with these terms?

One of the many reasons we love life in the South is that there is no more "dress for success" and best of all no pantyhose. Here it is dress for comfort. When I am old I will wear purple; right now I will wear whatever I want.

Our Florida attire is determined by the weather. Cooler weather may send us running to our closets for the seldom-used fleece and wool. Hot weather wear? Rule number one: Less is more—but the less has to be washed constantly. The hotter the weather the more loads of wash rumble in the laundry room. A sultry, humid day demands many costume changes. It might be golf or tennis duds, the gardening togs or casual run-around clothes. When we venture out, then we may adopt the ubiquitous "resort casual" apparel.

Today's easy wear/easy care clothing certainly does make life easier. Just toss it all in the washing machine. At our house if something can't go in the washing machine it doesn't last long. Our washer and dryer are in constant motion. We consider folding laundry exercise.

Like so many couples, when a social event arrives, we often end up in one of those classic "George and Grace/Ralph and Alice" conversations. Invariably, while trying to decide what to wear to a planned event, my husband enters the room. Then comes *the* question. "What should I wear?" he asks.

It is a classic no-win. Whatever my response, I can anticipate a counter response. But I never learn, so I say, "No jacket, fresh shirt, long pants, socks (and shoes), and take a tie just in case."

Then his Ralph to my Alice: "It is too hot. I bet nobody dresses up. I don't want to wear a jacket."

My Alice: "Then why do you ask? Wear what you want to."

Then we get there: "Why didn't you tell me guys would be wearing jackets?"

It is tougher for guys; the dress code is more rigid. It goes from shorts and polo shirts all the way to full penguin—the tuxedo. The girl dress code is much looser, but potentially more emotional. Not sure of an upcoming event, I play the costume game. Will I be black and sultry or cute and fresh? Do I wear a hat? I do like my hats. Once at the event, a quick look around the room and a huge sigh of relief when I find I am in sync.

Like every normal warm-blooded woman, I love a man in a tux. While most of the time we enjoy the easy, casual look, there are events that call for the full tuxedo. My husband knows some things are not negotiable, so when a formal event is on the calendar there is no discussion. He'll never admit it, but there is something magical and, yes, romantic about the classic black and white starchiness of a tuxedo.

Resort casual? I guess I like "resorting" to casual. After all, that is one of the reasons we live in Florida.

R.O.M.E.O.S

My seaside community has clubs of all kinds. Golfers have their country clubs. Tennis players have their groups. There is a variety of service clubs—Rotary, Kiwanis, Optimists, Shriners and Lions meet regularly. Clubs suit a purpose. They allow people with similar interests and goals to get together and do what they like to do. The service clubs in a community offer valuable volunteer time and revenue for worthy causes.

A very different kind of club meets every Wednesday morning at one of our local eateries. The club is called the "R.O.M.E.O.S" (Retired Old Men Eating Out). The group assembles at a long table reserved for them each Wednesday; they've been doing this for over three years. The group can be as few as five or six, or as many as fifteen or twenty. The rules are simple: Bring your good humor, life experiences and appetite. R.O.M.E.O.S has become an institution and a regularly scheduled part of its members' schedules.

Their clubhouse? A breakfast-eating kind of place that has been a long-time area favorite. Their usual waitress loves the group and her eyes sparkle as she takes orders from her regulars. She quickly goes around the table looking each man in the eye. A nod may mean "the usual" and she knows who gets the grits and sausage, who gets the oatmeal, and so on. She has nicknames for some of the members.

The club started when a group of retired men thought it might be fun to get together and have breakfast and enjoy some stimulating conversation—and most importantly, talk about anything but golf. In addition, many found that retirement and couple time together can be a bit too much for husbands and wives. They find that a little "guy time" is therapeutic.

Once R.O.M.E.O.S began meeting, their membership soon grew by word-of-mouth. The group is an interesting cross-pollination of life and career experiences; it includes an FBI agent, a radiologist, an airline pilot, an engineer, an insurance executive, and on and on. They clearly enjoy each other's company and their mornings out.

The early organizers imagined a group whose conversations would be lively and interesting, focusing on world news and weighty issues. That lasted only a couple of weeks. The focus changed quickly. These days, the ROMEOS find that they prefer exchanging information about local happenings, problem solving, and small town gossip—plus, of course, good old-fashioned grits and gravy breakfasts.

Beach Day

How many people can leave on vacation and arrive at their destination in ten minutes? Living on an island with the Atlantic Ocean at its easternmost border offers opportunities for instant vacations. People travel from all over the country to enjoy the beautiful Florida beaches, but all we have to do is jump in the car and drive a short distance.

It still takes some planning. First we pack up—water, chairs, towels, etc.; then there's usually a discussion as to whether or not to take the two Yorkshire Terriers. Usually I lose, and so do the dogs. For some reason panting dogs and leashes tangled around our beach chairs hold no appeal for my husband. We are sure to pack the sunscreen with SPF ranging from 8 to 24, plus of course, our hats. We usually load up our beach bag with our current reading projects—books, newspapers and magazines. Beach reading is different somehow and we enjoy it.

Arriving at the beach and parking the car, we unload and begin the walk across one of the many long boardwalks that lead to our seaside escape. We move across the weathered wood stretching over the dunes and are greeted with the first kiss of a cool breeze off the ocean. There is nothing like it.

We glance up and down the beach, with its unrivaled scrubbed-clean look, as we search for that perfect spot. We unpack towels, chairs and other supplies and settle in for the afternoon. We are soon lulled by the warm sun, gentle breezes and the slapping of sea on sand.

For two people who seldom slow down our forced relaxation is a treat. Beach outings usually include a walk for me. I meander along the fringe of the surf line watching for unexpected treasures offered up by the ocean. Small shells fill my pockets and will join many others collected through the years that inhabit jars and baskets throughout the house.

At home we are surrounded by sound. Each of us is guilty of hitting the television button as we enter a room. CNN and sporting events are a constant. Our beachside mini-vacations offer a pleasant contrast. The sounds there are all on low and the colors are muted. We enjoy the slow-motion entertainment all around us: small children building sandy fortresses; dogs racing into the sea to retrieve soggy tennis balls; earnest walkers moving quickly to some tune that drains from their earphones. Looking skyward we are entertained by planes pulling messages that encourage patronage of the local beach stores.

Our beach retreats are treasured, and as we head back to the sun-baked car we ask each other why we don't go on vacation more often.

Beach Teeth

Beach combing is addictive. If there is a beach near me, I am there. My bare feet have found sandy, and sometimes rocky beaches around the world. Once on a beach, the search begins for treasures the sea might have tossed to the shore.

The treasures collected through the years are mostly shells. The shells fill baskets, bowls and jars throughout our home. Some can be identified—what they are and where they were found. The amazing colors and sculpted shapes never cease to fascinate me.

The beaches near my Florida home call to me and I have developed a new obsession: sharks' teeth. Those who seek the ancient teeth of prehistoric creatures become addicted once they find their first tooth. We are now in the "the club" and now routinely find five or six during each trip to our secret spot.

What is it about sharks' teeth that so fascinate folks? There is a mystique about these ancient, fossilized teeth that draws us to the edge of the sea at low tide in hopes of finding one or two. The teeth might be the size of a pin or as large as five inches long. It is mind numbing to fathom that these teeth are relics from creatures that lived in the waters off our coast 10 to 50 million years ago.

Think about it. That is *really* old. Holding a hardened, shiny, earth-toned tooth, its serrated edges still intact, one can't help but be awestruck by the oddity of a shed tooth that has survived longer than we can even imagine. Every animal that walks, swims or flies has an ancestor that lived in the Ice Age. And the shark is one of the oldest.

Small wonder they survive. Sharks can reach a length of 70 feet, and an average shark produces 24,000 teeth in a decade. As a tooth is lost another moves forward to take its place. The largest teeth come from the megalodon shark, a predecessor of the great white shark.

There is a talent or charm to finding them. It has taken me many years to have any luck at all. What's the trick? Some seekers seem to have magical karma that leads them to the sharks' teeth, while others search and search with no luck.

A few tips: Low tide is best; smaller sharks' teeth are usually along the edge of the water among shells and pebbles; the very large carcharodon teeth are flung higher, and, because they are heavy, are buried quickly. You have to be quick.

Searching for sharks' teeth—another wonderful excuse to go to the beach.

FALL

The Snake That Came To Church

Living in the southern United States has many plusses. But as is often said, with the good comes the bad. We have snakes in our beautiful, sub-tropical, Florida paradise. Snakes are part of the lush, dense marshes that provide our stunning vistas.

Many believe that the only good snake is a dead snake. Not true. Snakes are not, of course, all bad. Snakes are an important part of our eco-system; without them, even more unwelcome creatures would proliferate and cause us even worse problems. Most local folks have a snake story or two.

Shortly after our move to Northeast Florida, my husband was passing through our screened porch on his way to the barbecue that sits on the patio below. He noticed what he thought was a coiled rope in the corner. Wondering why I had acquired a length of rope as thick as the coils you see on ocean-going ships, he nonetheless proceeded with his barbecue project. Hamburgers sizzling on the grill, he returned to fetch the oversized coil of rope. It moved! The "rope" was actually a very large rat snake, which we later found to be harmless.

His call from the porch had me running to see what was wrong. I was instructed to get a broom and shovel and to HURRY. My first reaction… I was wearing the wrong shoes. Looking down at my feet in their open-toed sandals, my instincts were to change into shoes or boots that offered more protection. We later chuckled at my concern about the proper shoes to wear when fighting a snake.

Tools in hand, I returned to fight the good battle with my brave partner. We were able to chase the huge snake out the back door and back into the marsh behind the house. The battle won, we looked at each other and acknowledged a whole new level of respect for the verdant paradise we call home.

On a recent Sunday, sitting in our church sanctuary, we settled in to listen to a well-crafted sermon prepared by our pastor. We look forward to his thoughtful and scholarly sermons. Fully enveloped in the serenity of that peaceful Sunday morning, we were suddenly aware that something unusual was happening. It seems an unexpected and unwelcome visitor was determined to interrupt the service. A four-foot snake slithered across the stage area, temporarily halting the sermon as several ushers rushed to the front, brooms in hand.

The snake removed, our pastor looked out to his congregation and chuckled. He remarked that in all his years at the pulpit this was a first. With his trademark humor, he reminded us that snakes as symbols of temptation and evil are not unknown in church circles; but, perhaps this was going a bit too far. The incident brought giggles from the congregation as they made their way to their cars.

Our instinctive reaction to snakes is one of aversion and fear. Our Bible-based beliefs lead us to think of snakes as serpents symbolizing the dark side; but our recent, unexpected visitor appeared to be harmless. The snake taught us once again to look beyond our first instinctive thoughts of good and evil.

Her-icane

It happens every year – hurricane season. We are reminded daily of the status of current or potential tropical storms and hurricanes. It's part of the bargain we make living on the coast of Florida. The names never cease to amuse me. In the first place, why is it a "her"icane and not a "him"icane? I can hear it now—it is because we women stir up so much trouble.

A few years ago we worked our way through the alphabet and arrived at the letter "I". The storm's name? Isidore. Isidore? Who thought that up? It did not get better, as names for the storms that might follow included Kyle, Lili, Marco and Nana. Then it got even more intriguing—Omar and Paloma were slated to go down in weather history.

Until 1978 storm names were exclusively female. It seems that the use of women's names started on the other side of the world, in Australia of all places. We can blame Clement Wragge, an Australian meteorologist, who began giving women's names to storms at the end of the 19th century. Whatever could Mrs. Wragge have done to cause Clement to make such a move? We can only wonder.

During World War II both the Navy and Air Force found that women's names were a convenient way to identify storms. Evidently, the use of names made it easier to keep track of all the different storms that might be active simultaneously. Women might find it comforting that the most devastating hurricane to hit Florida so far has been Andrew, a man's name.

As it turns out there is quite a protocol in the storm naming game. A storm is worthy of naming when it reaches wind speed of 39 miles per hour—it is then a tropical storm, which may grow to hurricane-hood. Names are alphabetical with the exception of X, Y and Z, which are not used. Names are reused with one exception: If a storm is especially deadly or economically devastating the name is retired.

I think it might be fun to name them after actual people like Elvis, Madonna, Tiger or maybe Prince (who was once known, ironically, as the artist who shall remain unnamed).

Our move to Florida from the Midwest meant a change from concern about tornados or the dreaded "winter storm watch" to monitoring storms as they develop in the warm waters surrounding Florida. Tornados are deadly and come with little warning. At least hurricanes give us time to prepare.

When the H word comes up at our house we usually decide it is time to check the green plastic tub that sits high on a shelf in the garage. We call it the Hurricane Box. If a storm threatens we do an inventory. If checked against the lists of emergency essentials offered by the media we probably would score 50%. We do have water, flashlights, a radio and batteries. What we consider essentials are not on most basic survival lists. Our list includes white wine, dog food and Peanut M & Ms.

Each resident of our island has a tale about the 1999 Great Evacuation Adventure when hurricane Floyd threatened the coast of Florida, and specifically, our Island. We were ordered to evacuate. I can still picture some weatherman, hair blowing in the wind, valiantly hanging onto a vibrating stop sign and mumbling something about an approaching storm bigger than the state of Texas.

Although it was sunny and clear at the time, near panic broke out as our community packed up and headed for safety. People remembered hurricane Andrew and the devastation it did to Dade County in 1992. Our household waited until the last minute. We evacuated all of 12 miles, spending the night in a nearby town, sleeping in our car with our Yorkshire terrier.

Our experience was not even in the finals of those we heard over the next few weeks. Clearly, many of those who fled would have preferred to stay in a roofless house, knee-deep in water, rather than face the traffic and headaches that the last-minute evacuation delivered.

So check that Hurricane Box and be prepared. You just never know.

Grandparents

If only we could go back in time and talk to the grandparents now long gone. For most of us the images and memories of them come from vague stories and photos seen on walls and in albums. But there is so much we can never know. What made them laugh? What did they like to eat? What were their dreams and hopes?

I would like to spend time with my grandparents—all four long gone. They led amazing, adventuresome lives, yet all that is left is bits and pieces. I look through old boxes and albums, trying desperately to organize, and at the same time, find just a small piece of the true essence of these ancestors.

Even my parents and their youth remain a mystery. As I envision the paintings and pictures that populated my parents many homes, I remember the striking black and white portrait of a handsome couple on their wedding day. I recall a pastel portrait of my mother with my sister and me, maybe eight and ten years old, and photos of elegant men and women in aged sepia staring back.

I can only digest small bits and pieces of the past. Each time I visited my father in another of his apartments, which got smaller and smaller, I would go to the trunk that now resides in my guest bedroom and sort through memorabilia. Like an urn of ashes, the trunk is all that is left of my four grandparents. Now, each time I dig through that ancient trunk I find surprises and pieces fitting into the puzzles of their lives.

It is a shame that an interest in our grandparents comes to us when we are in the later years of our own life experiences. When we are young, just beginning our lives, we have little curiosity or patience with those that came before us. We look forward. In fact, we are impatient with their old fashioned ideas and are convinced that they cannot understand what we might be thinking or planning to do with our lives.

During my last "time trip" into the treasure-laden trunk, I found a box containing a carefully folded, crinkled and yellowed, seven-page document I had never seen before. It was typed—which in itself looks so odd in this age of electronic word processing. The words in my life are mostly on a screen, looking almost sterile. "Word processing"—even the term is stern and military sounding. The documents we deal with today lack the character of these crinkly, old pages from my trunk.

Removing the rusted paperclip, I began to read a program introduction about my maternal grandfather, written in his fifty-fifth year, at the peak of his professional success. My memory of my grandfather is of a very tall, quiet man with piercing, brown eyes. He certainly did not know what to do when his two granddaughters came to visit. Like my grandmother, he was an only child, as was my mother. Two busy little girls seemed a bit strange in his usually ordered world. He liked to play cards, watch wrestling and baseball on television, and loved to fish. As a child, I would go into his room and look at the shiny, black and white photos of him holding up huge fish caught in the Northwest. He smiled in those pictures taken a long time ago, but my memories are not of him smiling, especially after my grandmother died.

The grandfather of my memories came alive to me in the words I read in that old document. Who would have thought that this quiet, old man who sat for hours in his special chair, staring at a blinking television, could have led such an adventurous life? He left home at sixteen, determined to help build the Panama Canal. When he reached Galveston, Texas, where he would be transported to the canal construction site, he took one look at the men returning with malaria and yellow fever, and tore up his contract. He lived all over the country and eventually traveled the world.

What amazed me most about this bright, highly successful executive with Pacific Bell Telephone is that his career was interrupted by repeated trips to the deserts of California in search of gold. He went three times and each time returned empty-handed, finally focusing on his lifelong career with the telephone company. I wish I could ask him about his gold seeking adventures.

The adventures did not end for my grandparents when their retirement years approached. They accepted an assignment in Istanbul, Turkey. They sold their house, and moved to a primitive country where my grandfather was charged with helping the Turkish government modernize its archaic, inefficient telephone service. They used those years to travel further; one favorite old photo shows the two of them sitting on a pair of sullen big-lipped camels.

Glimpses into the lives of my grandparents make me wish that I had the chance to ask them the many questions that haunt me. I wish that I could have gotten to know those fascinating people—people who wrote wonderful, long, newsy letters; saved photographs; and took off to find gold in the deserts of California. Today I truly treasure the scraps of their lives that live in that dusty, old trunk in my guest room.

Last Parent

The phone rings and once again there is distressing news about an aging parent. You shut down your real-time life and hurry to do what you can to bring help and comfort. You wonder if this will be the final trip. There were many such calls during the last year of my father's life. Sometimes it was a fall; sometimes yet another trip to the hospital. There won't be any more; he died March 7, 2003, just short of his 90th birthday.

We've all heard it: Some deaths are a blessing. My father's death was a blessing. A proud and dignified man who never quite recovered from his wife's death is now at peace.

We talk so much about quality of life, but what about quality of death? It became more and more difficult to watch the struggle for life when we knew death would bring final release. That tough old man wasn't about "letting go," and we had to respect that. He made every decision right up until the last.

Strange, the words we choose to use when talking about death. We avoid the words "die" and "death." Instead, we talk about "losing someone," or we say someone is "gone." They aren't lost and they aren't gone. "Passing" is a better term, as death is truly a passing.

As the final weeks and days went by I experienced what so many of us do. The child becomes the parent. Spooning applesauce into the mouth of the frail and failing man, who barely resembled the handsome, dashing father I remember, became routine. I heard myself muttering the same encouraging words I once used with my young sons. I brushed his dentures and helped him to the bathroom. Someone said to me, as I lamented the emaciated shadow of a man that slipped away, to remember that everyone in heaven is 30. I like that.

As the last days passed I fell into a routine. Walking from the hospital parking lot, I passed the cheerful lady in the pink smock who greeted me each morning on my way to Dad's room. The small community hospital bustled with activity. I sensed that the employees truly cared about their patients.

There were no dramatic deathbed conversations with my father. Instead, we who have survived him will trust that the love we knew in our hearts was there, though we would have liked to have heard it from his lips. He wasn't one to compliment. He was quicker to make a cutting remark than one of praise. He showed his love through his loyalty, his support, and by example.

So now I have moved up in line. I try not to worry about what my children will have to deal with as my own wheels come off. Please grant me dignity and laughter, and a gentle passing.

Back home again, before catching up with the busy life I left behind, I was drawn to the beach. My father loved nothing more than sand between his toes and the comforting rhythm of the ocean, so I made my way to the water and thought of him.

The first of many stabs I knew would come came too quickly. Walking in the door upon my return home I instinctively went to the phone to call Dad and tell him that I was home, safe and sound.

I guess he knows.

Jackie O

Do clothes make a person? The Corcoran Gallery of Art in Washington, D.C., featured a special exhibit of clothing worn by Jacqueline Kennedy during her 1000 days as America's First Lady. During a visit to our nation's capital, I stepped out of a beautiful, crystal clear, early fall afternoon into the austere and stately halls of the Corcoran Gallery. Joined by a friend who lives in Washington, I had decided to take in the exhibit showcasing the gowns and state affair apparel worn by Mrs. Kennedy, the world-renowned fashion icon.

We paid for our tickets and treated ourselves to earphones to maximize our experience. Soldier-like mannequins were dressed in suits, gowns or dresses—always simple, always a beautiful color. Using our earphone sets, we would press the number corresponding to the number on the display in front of which we stood. We could hear music and voices from those years gone by. Behind each mannequin, a dramatic poster mural showed Jackie wearing the garment displayed. The recorded narration would tell us about the occasion, the designer's intention and rationale as to choice of color, skirt length, fabric and silhouette. Each description emphasized the effect that Jackie's carefully planned choice of clothing had on an event—some subtle and some not. The designer, Oleg Cassini, explained the intentional choice of sun colors for a visit to Mexico, and a classic, long, black dress, with a black lace mantilla, for a visit to the Vatican.

My friend and I were transported back in time in many ways. One was very personal. Seeing a proper, beautifully crafted suit worn with simple pumps, gloves and hat, took us back to the times, as young girls, when we attended church in dress, coat, gloves and hat. In a more dramatic way, seeing pictures and the actual garments of the former First Lady took us back to a magical time in our country's history—a time called "Camelot" by some.

The exhibit and detailed information provided was reflective of the grace and elegance of its subject. It was all about the quiet, intelligent charm of a very young (only 31) Jacqueline Bouvier Kennedy. Somehow none of the horror of her husband's assassination or the legacy of his dark side spoiled the experience.

We saw beautiful colors, and, yes, lots of the First Lady's favored pink. But we did *not* see the pink suit that is forever burned in our memories. We saw only the dresses, suits, ball gowns and coats that she must have been so very proud of—works of art in their own way, living art. My friend and I agreed that we would like to think of those times as happy times for Jackie. We hoped she had some sense of how very successfully she represented our country with her unique charm and élan.

As we moved along each display, the continuity achieved by Jackie's designers became evident—a continuing theme of simple, classic elegance, with subtle changes and details that offered new interest. Each accessory, whether it was a hat, jewelry, shoes or gloves, enhanced the overall effect.

You had to feel a bit sorry for the sometimes dowdy wives of the other diplomats and world leaders, who were often out-shown by the handsome young woman. "Jackie O," as she later became known, bravely chose to use her public persona to celebrate simple elegance, and yet, in her time, was criticized for extravagance. It took a brave and talented woman to spend the time and resources, and to expose herself to public disapproval and criticism with such style.

Do clothes make the person? In this case, an amazing woman, Jacqueline Kennedy, *made* the clothes.

Family Kayaking

Three sons, two wives and a new girl friend. One rare weekend when the entire family was in one place at one time we decided to do a family kayak outing. Unlike golf, tennis and other activities that break us into smaller groups, this was an opportunity to do something together.

Having made arrangements with a local outfitter, we met at a creek not far from the house. We piled out of our cars and joined at the dock where we were met by our guides for the day. The majority of the group had some experience, but we also had some first-timers.

We gathered for the prerequisite group photo, and then listened attentively to the basic instructions from one of our three guides. Life jackets were handed out. After a chorus of clicking and clacking as jacket buckles were secured, we gathered at the edge of the creek where the brightly colored kayaks awaited us.

One by one we climbed into our kayaks and were pushed out into the dark creek water. The weather had been teasing us, first looking like a possible washout, but then gifting us with a sunlit day.

Our crafts were red, yellow and green, and our apparel was a motley mix of colors and logos. We gathered like multihued water bugs waiting for the rest of the kayakers to join us.

Our ever-competitive group waited impatiently in the water for a signal. Paddles began to flick at the dark surface and we were off. After some preliminary thrashing each of us found our own rhythm. We glided forward without colliding with fellow water rats or any other challenges the creek offered up.

We passed under a bridge alive with the rumble of cars. We left the hum and hassle of the highway behind and fell into our own unique methods of forward motion.

As we moved along in the quiet of that late November afternoon, we were reminded of past water adventures that have ranged from white water rafting down the Colorado River to windsurfing off the coast of Delaware. Our family water memories are mostly good ones.

Skeletons of trees that had dropped their leaves and tropical plants growing randomly and wildly through the dense woods bordered the still waters. The quiet added to the serene stage set as we passed in review. We glided past homes tucked in the woods, with their prerequisite docks, but no signs of people. We thought we heard harmonica music. The creek twisted and turned. Fallen trees, old docks and sunken logs tested our kayaking skills.

The kayak is easy to maneuver—a calm mind and an instinctive dip of the paddle can set you right fairly quickly. Our guides' helpful tips were kept in mind: sit up straight; remember that your head should stay within the perimeter of your kayak.

The water appeared dense. The tannin so darkened the creek's water that it looked like a sheet of blackened glass, the reflection startling clear. It was difficult to tell what was real and what was reflected. We sensed that the water was not deep, but no one wanted to test it.

Then it was time to return. Too soon we could hear the sound of the highway and its rude reminder that we were nearing the end of our outing. We climbed out of our kayaks, proud of our family adventure into the deep, watery woods. We shared the euphoria that fresh air, physical exertion and time together can bring. We patted ourselves on the back, climbed into our cars and headed home for hot showers, cold drinks and a family meal.

Garage Sales

On any given Saturday the streets of our town are invaded. Saturday morning is garage sale time. Neighborhoods are clogged with bargain hunters looking for the best deals. Eager shoppers jump out of cars clutching a list of garage sales that appeared in Wednesday's newspaper.

I don't think they have garage sales in other countries. They have market day, jumbles or flea markets, but not what appears to be an American tradition—the garage sale. Come to think of it, I don't think folks in other countries are quite the packrats we Americans are.

We have all done it – the garage sale thing. Once you place that ad in the paper you are committed, but the process begins weeks before the sale. And it is quite a process. In the case of our garage sales, the dining room became the dedicated holding area. All kinds of things get piled there. Checking it periodically I find that my spouse and I do not always agree. I try to add one of his worthless (but treasured) possessions to the pile on the table. He takes it back. He would ask why something of mine was not included and begrudgingly I add it to the pile. So the glacier grows.

A word to the wise: In the case of garage sales, quick decisions are good decisions. Trust me, you will never miss it. Determine that an item is no longer useful to anyone near and dear, then put it in the designated holding area and never, never look back. Yes, it is hard. If you linger you are lost. Once you retrieve one item you may trigger a flood that reverses all of your good work. Remember, the goal is that the garage sale inventory pile should grow, not get smaller.

The day of the sale soon arrives. At first light, with cup of coffee in hand, we pull the sheets off the goodies we hope to sell—various piles representing the remnants of other lives in other places; duplicates of things; gifts received but never used; and so on.

Pick-up trucks and cars park waiting for the signal that they can shop. It is a cult—the folks that come at the crack of dawn waiting for the bell to ring. The more seasoned and semi-professionals quickly scan the assortment of items, make their decisions, pay, and without so much as eye contact or a smile, are off to the next garage sale.

"Less is more, less is more," I remind myself, as people purchase the odd-lot pile of goods along our driveway. There are moments of regret, but I stand firm and enjoy the feel of dollars and quarters in my pocket.

The later shoppers are usually more gregarious and seem to be going from sale to sale for the fun of it. They stop to chat and even say nice things about some of the leftovers, but they do not buy. While my back is turned I hear my husband say, "Just take it." He knows… out of sight, out of mind.

When the sale is over the orphans look pretty sad. A promise is made to my husband that whatever did not sell would go to our local charity store. He knows me too well. The car is packed and gone before I have a chance to even think about retrieving some of those unclaimed treasures. And we don't miss them— the three tennis racquets, the old golf clubs, those piles of books, battered baskets, pots, pans and tools, that old VCR… and on and on.

Yes, I too had a time in my life where I would brake for garage sales. Great bargains were to be found, but more often than not the "treasures" ended up offered at my next garage sale.

WINTER

Unexpected Gifts

Who doesn't like to receive an unexpected gift? They come to us in many different ways. I feel blessed to live in a community small enough that the daily pace of life includes time taken to give unexpected gifts. Look for them and be thankful. Better yet, be the giver instead of the getter.

We have all been disappointed at one time or another when a special day has come and gone and we haven't been remembered. Sometimes even a mother forgets a birthday—mine did. As families grow through marriages, grandchildren and great-grandchildren, there are more and more red-letter days to remember.

On top of that, we are deluged with forced holidays, such as Secretaries' Day, and, of course, Bosses' Day. The creativity of marketers is endless. Have you noticed that we are always between holidays? You send out valentines only to find the card shops full of St. Patrick's Day cards. What follows Halloween and Thanksgiving? The granddaddy of all gift-giving days, Christmas. It never ends.

Why not remember a *non*-red-letter day—just a day when you want to express your love or friendship or empathy? The gift doesn't have to be a prettily wrapped box or a lavish bouquet of flowers. A simple card or a telephone call can be the best present of all.

Gifts can come in different forms. Every day brings unexpected gifts.

It is a gift when you are lost and someone stops to give you directions, or you struggle to find the right coins and a stranger behind you comes up with the missing change. Caught in busy traffic, someone stops and waves you in with a smile. Out of the blue, someone compliments you on a haircut or what you are wearing that day.

Something simple—given for no special reason—can be a true and special gift. A favorite at my house is an unanticipated bouquet of flowers waiting on the kitchen counter—"just because."

One day an extraordinary, unexpected gift came my way. It started with a kindness done for a wonderful and talented friend, and resulted in a totally surprising gift—an outrageous, extravagant, black feather boa that she knew I coveted, but felt I couldn't buy. That unexpected gift will keep on giving. Every time I wear it I will be reminded of my friend, and the fluffy feathers will always carry a special kind of loving energy when I wrap them around my neck.

So take time out from all the commercialization of this or that holiday. Just give something simple to someone who may need a little gift. And who knows? This may be your day when a gift comes your way—totally unexpected.

Forever Friends

Friendships are the glue that keep many of us together in the roughest of times and add spice and joy to our lives in the best of times. They are the cream in our coffee, nuts on our sundae... no, I am not going to break into song. But I am going to get a little emotional about friendship. So much has been written about friendship and its power in our lives. It is difficult to try to say it in a new and different way.

Friendships come in all shapes, sizes, depths and widths. Friendships are struck as we move through our lives and sometimes when we least expect it. They happen with people who come as surprises—pleasant ones. Friendships come as we involve ourselves in careers, our children's activities and spouse's work. There are tennis and golf friends; friends who love to read and share their books and thoughts; friends who love the beauty, birds and blooms that abound in our neighborhoods. There are friends that we work with side by side as we volunteer in our community. There are girl friends and boy friends and couple friends.

Then there are "forever friends." A recent weekend spent with such a friend reinforced and nourished our "forever friendship." We finish each other's sentences—always have. We laugh at each other and the silly and even stupid things we do. These forever friends are a little different. That is not to say all friends are not forever, but we all have those special friends in our lives who are somehow just, well, extraordinary.

We can have more than one forever friend. Some of us are blessed to be married to a forever friend. I am. Not only do we finish each other's sentences, but sometimes we say the same thing at the same time. Reading is a shared passion. When a new book we were both interested in came out recently we bought it for each other on the same day. Talk about being in sync.

The weekend reunion with my old and forever friend began with an instant connection, as if no time had passed since we last shared a big piece of time together. We have history, as they say. Divorces, children's triumphs and disasters, deaths of parents and our own struggles with careers and relationships—all shared through the years. We say things out loud to each other that we would dare not say to anyone else. We challenge and are challenged.

It *is* about us and that's okay. We chuckle as we recall the battles fought and mostly won, but not always. Thoughts bounce back and forth freely between true forever friends. The honesty can be brutal, but it is from the heart. True friends tell you what you don't want to hear, but probably need to hear.

Gifts between forever friends are from the heart and always right on. They bring smiles and are often something you would have picked yourself.

Forever friends know when to send flowers, when to call, when to be there and when to back off. Forever friends laugh at each other and with each other. When they are together they dig deeper and freely explore every corner of their souls.

Treasure your "forever friends" and count your blessings.

Clean House?

Cleaning house is not my thing. A friend suggested that the whole pointless process of cleaning house might make a good column. Chuckling, she mentioned hearing someone once say that cleaning house is like stringing beads with no knot at the end of the string. So why string?

I would rather do than maintain. My choice is to be outside in the sunshine and not in my house dusting. That has always been my way. The move to Florida has made it easier to indulge my wandering ways. Back in the Midwest where I spent so many years, it was a little tough to be outside in February when twelve inches of snow lay on the cold hard ground and the wind chill took the temperature well below zero.

Remember mudrooms? A mudroom was part of every house I ever lived in. Growing up, that's where we shed jackets, mittens and boots as we came in the back door after school. As my boys grew up, wet, muddy or snowy boots were left in piles, often mingled with wet mittens and soggy, wool hats. As if it were yesterday I can close my eyes and remember the smoky smell of damp clothing drying near a radiator.

There are tradeoffs, always. While we Floridians may not deal with mud and snow, we do have to deal with sand from the beach and clay from tennis courts. My husband, also known as "the saint," is in charge of the vacuum cleaner. He takes his job very seriously. He often stands sentinel when I return from the beach or the tennis court, reminding me to take off the offending shoes so that I do not leave a trail of sand or clay.

Most would agree cleaning a house without children should be an easier task, but so many find that retired husbands may leave their own trail of newspapers and golf paraphernalia. In those days of small children and multiple pets, my days were filled with harvesting cat and dog fur and endless baseball caps left by my own boys and their entourage of friends. A dreaded task was trying to assign chores. It would've been easier to herd cats, as I recall. I don't miss that.

Cleaning house has it's compensations. I do like the homey smells of cleaning: the oily, lemony smell of furniture polish as it is massaged into wood furniture; the gritty, powdery smell of Soft Scrub as it works to remove stains from sinks and tubs; the stringent smell of neon blue Windex as it dribbles down the windows waiting to be whisked away by a clean paper towel; the institutional smell of Pine-Sol as it marinates in a bucket of tepid water waiting for the mop. The scents combine into a unique potpourri—the essence of clean.

Most need incentives and deadlines to kick us into housecleaning mode. Houseguests and dinner parties certainly get us moving. Houseguests beg a deeper clean—more rooms and under beds. With dinner guests you can close doors. When we entertain, things are pushed into cupboards and closets often never to be found again.

From The Porch

Dirt is one thing but dust is another. Dirt we keep under control. Dust seems to replace itself after each housecleaning campaign. I always loved the story of the little boy who listened earnestly as his mother explained that we start as dust and we end as dust. Later the youngster pulled at his mother's skirt and worriedly told her that someone was coming and going under his bed.

So I will try and do better, but if the sun is shining you know where I'll be.

Girl Friend Birthday

A group of women gathered one cool, windy February morning to commemorate landmark birthdays—two among us celebrated 65 years within a few weeks of each other. Time for a party, we all agreed.

Yes, these two were getting older, but, more importantly, they truly were getting better. Both celebrated with sass and smiles. If this is what 65 looks like I'm not so worried. Age and how we look at it is a funny phenomenon. When we are little, we measure each year in shorter increments. You ask a small child how old he is and he proudly says, "I'm 4 *and a half*." Remember how long those years between birthday parties used to seem? Ask a teenager how old she is and you will find her eager to be grown up, probably saying, "Almost 16." Almost 16 is most likely closer to 14.

When someone asks me my age I have to hesitate. It's not that I choose to hide my age. It's more that as the years fly by faster and faster I truly do not remember.

As we planned our girlfriend birthday celebration, there was no mention of black balloons or the dark side of getting older. These birthday girls are much loved and stand as wonderful role models in our community.

They embrace life with total enthusiasm. Giving back may be what we admire the most about the two who were feted that day. They have enriched our community, but each would argue that it is they who have been enriched.

The seasoned group had great fun laughing at and with each other. Old friends enjoyed our time together and some new friendships were begun. Roasts and toasts brought emotions ranging from tears to clapping and laughing. We heard some wonderfully silly stories about our birthday girls, which made them even more human and lovable, and, yes, like us.

We were reminded that the passing years have given us beautiful memories and very special friends who *knew us when,* and who can share the funny, life-affirming stories that bring smiles and tears. We celebrated friends present, friends absent, and, each in our own way, friends from other times and places.

There is something about being on the other side of 50. We all agree we have earned some good times and enjoy them with gusto. We worry less and less about how we look or what we have. What is more important is how we feel and how we make other people feel. There are so many things we don't have to do anymore, and we smile patiently as our children fuss about car pools, house payments, sassing kids, and managing too many things in too little time. We have been there and don't have to be there any more. We have earned our pasture.

Our celebration was leisurely. We didn't have to rush to get somewhere. We moved through the golden day with great pleasure, embracing each treasured moment. We all left feeling like we had made new friends and celebrated the joy of being women in our golden years.

There were giggles and tears and lunch and cake. We all laughed about how 65 used to sound so old, but not anymore—it is just the beginning. There is no reason not to do anything we want to do. We may be a little slower and it may take a little longer, but why not try?

Why do we choose to fuss over folks we love on their birthdays? Because it makes us stop and take the time to express how very glad we are that they were born and are in our lives.

Grandma Wannabe

There are lots of us. We are ready, willing and able to accept the gleeful challenges of grandmother-hood, but find ourselves without little ones. Our children have delayed marriage, and, yes, delayed having families. So we find ourselves in a frustrating situation that we cannot do too much about—living without grandchildren. I am ready, but clearly my children are not. Two are happily married, even have houses and dogs, but are in no hurry to fulfill my dream. My two married sons smile indulgently and my beloved daughters-in-law just roll their eyes.

These grandchildren of my dreams can call me anything they want. Granny, Grandma, Grandmama or Grandmother. They can call me Grandma Trot-Trot, as one friend is called by her herd of grandchildren. My mother fretted over what her first grandchild would call her and chose her own designation: "Nani." It stuck, and Nani she was to her three adoring grandsons. My father was not concerned about what he would be called, but was a bit surprised when his first grandson, vocal and eager to please at an early age, got the grandparent thing a bit mixed up. He called his grandfather "Grandma Daddy"—it worked.

Auntie Mame is my role model, outrageous and proud of it. This grandma will eat dessert first, go barefoot, ignore bedtimes and eat ice cream for breakfast, which, come to think of it is what I do now.

I know right where the dusty box is that holds the treasured childhood classics waiting for the next generation. Dr. Seuss, Winnie the Pooh, Wind in the Willows, Alice in Wonderland—they will just have to wait. Knitting needles stand ready to click busily as they produce tiny sweaters and caps out of soft, pastel yarns. I do not have a grandbaby hope chest like one friend, but I am tempted.

Grand *dogs* don't count, as much as I love all three of mine. Knitting for dogs just doesn't cut it. I have suggested to my children that these lovable dogs clearly need children to play with—a reversal of the usual new puppy or kitten for the children.

There is a gleam of hope. My best bet looks like my youngest. He and his wife are settled in a cozy, little suburban home, with two dogs. They just bought a new station wagon. A nice *family* car, I comment. Hey, I may be grasping, but at least I have resisted the urge to send them a baby seat for the new car.

We grandma wannabes take little solace from our friends who try to comfort us as they tuck their latest photos of their grandbabies back into their purses. "Oh, they will all come at once," they say. Easy for them to say. "Be careful what you wish for," reminds another, who is still exhausted from a week of grandchildren visiting. She has the glassy-eyed look of one who has had too much DisneyWorld, and too many beach outings, video games and fast food.

To heck with those daughter-in-law biological clocks. Mine is ticking. Please let me a grandmother before I am the one in diapers.

Holiday Hoopla

Every holiday season I ask the same question: Why do we do this to ourselves? There is a bit of the "bah humbug" in me. I have to work harder and harder to find the true spirit of Christmas.

Christmas *hoopla* seems to come earlier and earlier each year and I resent it. Where are the Christmas police? They should arrest anyone selling Christmas trees and holiday decorations before Thanksgiving and certainly before Halloween.

It all seems to get diluted—too much too soon and far too long. Guilt screams at us from our televisions, newspapers and magazines. Shopping malls are crowded with frantic shoppers. And what do we see in the advertising charging at us from every direction? Beautiful presents being exchanged by beautiful families—no divorce, no dogs throwing up, no grandparents with Alzheimer's, no unemployed dads, and no lost cats or kids with chicken pox. Instead, we see rosy-cheeked youngsters, with smiling grandparents, and the super-mom pulling it all off—dinner for twenty and perfect gifts for each and everyone.

The Christmases of my youth were slower and subtler. Our tree went up Christmas Eve. Part of the magic of Christmas was finding a decorated tree the next morning with presents all around. Our Santa back then was one clever guy. Now trees are up for months, not just days or weeks. Not only that, you can buy synthetic trees that pop out of a box and are already strung with lights. Imagine no pine needles in the car, no tangled tree lights, no trying to find the "bad" light or getting the tree to stand straight. Easier, yes, but I miss the piney fresh smell of the real thing and the charm of an asymmetrical tree.

And the gift thing. Every year I search for another way. Tension and stress begin to accelerate around Thanksgiving week. Lists are made. We promise not to give gifts, but end up doing it anyway. We have adopted a name drawing tradition in our family to ensure receiving one really nice gift instead of stuff for the garage sale pile. It seems to work pretty well.

I like the handmade and homemade—especially those that are edible. Baking the cookies and preparing the nibble recipes that I connect with Christmas do bring me some Christmas cheer. I just need to stay out of the malls, I guess.

To me it is about children and lights. Yes, lights. Lights are quiet and they don't yell at you; they recall other Christmases. When it is dark in balmy Florida and you see holiday lights, you can imagine the snow of your Christmas dreams.

Trying to find a kinder, gentler Christmas? Get in your car one dark night, play a tape of classic Christmas carols, and go on a Christmas light treasure hunt. You will be rewarded.

When it is all said and done, the very best way to find Christmas is through a child. If you do not have one close at hand, find one and share the magic.

Dog's Eye View of the Holidays

It's our turn. Everyone likes the "Porch" stories, but it's time you learn that the porch has dogs living on it too. And we have our own stories. This is our chance to give readers a slightly different perspective. In our case, it's from about twelve inches off the floor. There are two of us and we are proud little Yorkshire Terriers and usually get our way, but not during the holidays. So here is a dog's eye view of what the holidays do to our lives. It isn't pretty.

It gets insane at our house. Our humans are out of control. We're thinking maybe it's time they go to obedience school. A shock collar may be just the thing to settle them down. What can we say? There is no consistent discipline.

Our house by the marsh is ordinarily very quiet, but not in December. It all starts when they bring a tree into the house. Yes, a regular old tree. Then they put it on a table by the window. Now tell me what good does that do us? We can't use it like an outdoor tree. Very frustrating.

So now we have a live tree on the table. The next thing they do is put lights on it—little white lights. Then they open other boxes and pull out all kinds of strange things. Many look like good chew toys, but we never get a chance to check them out.

For some reason there is a lot more food around this time of year. Morsels get dropped on the floor and we do our best to help clean up. We find ourselves muttering to each other, "I've got to stop eating and get more exercise. I've put on some weight. I must be close to seven pounds. I have *never* weighed seven pounds!"

The strange December rituals continue. Packages are brought into the house and then wrapped in bright paper with ribbons tied all around. Once they are all wrapped up, they are put on the table with that blinking tree decorated with forbidden "chew toys".

Ordinarily we are together as a family in the evenings, often eating our dinner in front of the TV. For weeks the humans go out every night and do not even think about taking us along. But… just when we were sure that our lives had already changed forever comes the strangest ritual of all.

One dark, cool evening all the candles around the house are lit and loud music flows from the music system. Everyone stares at the chew toy tree with all its packages. Then something sets off the humans. Suddenly the paper is pulled off the presents and thrown onto the floor. We have fun chasing it. There were all kinds of *oohs* and *ahs* and hugs. Everyone seemed very happy. We even get presents. We like toys and get some wonderful, fresh ones.

After all of the presents are opened things quiet down and folks admire their gifts. We each find a warm lap where we settle down. We hope that this odd ritual marks the end of all the irregularity in our lives.

It takes a few days, but the decorations and lights are taken off the tree and it is taken out to the curb for the trash men to take away. All the boxes and gifts disappear.

We welcome the return to our regular schedule of morning walks, and a quiet house with family time in front of the TV. Thank heavens this only happens once a year—December is hard on dogs.

Christmas Hangover

Each year, following the high tension of the holiday season, I look forward to the comfort of life's normal ebb and flow. As we settle back into our schedules we spend some time reflecting. How did we do? Were our gifts successful? Were we surprised by a very special, unexpected gift? How many holiday cards did we get from people we did not send them to? How many Christmas letters did we receive? How many of those people did we really want to know so much about? Did we contribute something that was not about us, but, instead, about someone who truly needed help and hope?

The days after each holiday season are like recovering from a bad cold—a hangover of sorts. We are eager to get back to a routine and feel good again. A dreaded cold slows you down, forces you to pay attention to it and takes you out of your regular routine. Don't get me wrong. Unlike a bad cold, the holidays bring wonderful, unexpected and precious moments; but, to me anyway, they are something to get through.

Each of us has cherished moments to savor. During one Christmas of recent memory, it was the visit of my 87-year-old father that prompted the simple pleasures of nightly fires in the fireplace, and gentle memories of my mother—whose loss still stung. Also treasured was the special effort made by our busy children and their families to share time with their grandfather and with us.

We have implemented a simplified gift exchange, hopeful that we can lessen the financial and logistical burden while improving the quality of our Secret Santa's gift. Each family member picks out and purchases a single, hopefully, truly wonderful and personal gift.

The first year of this gift exchange idea, we declared it a success and enjoyed some unexpected bonus moments. We had an interesting combination of Secret Santas and recipients. My newly married son drew his wife's name and she drew his! The gift to her was a coveted sewing machine; his was an airline ticket to join his brothers on a ski vacation.

My gift? From a daughter-in-law to be, a beach walking sweater, but with a bonus— the security tag was still attached. Our quick-witted group teased our newest family member about the morality of shoplifting her future mother-in-law's Christmas gift. My sometimes playfully rowdy boys will not soon forget this most joke inducing of all gifts.

My treasured Christmas moments? Seeing my softened and somewhat frail father with his full-of-life, world-conquering grandsons sharing *thens* and *nows*; wonderful times with friends and their temporarily expanded families; and, chuckling at the electrical yard art—the best and worst of eccentric uses for strings of lights. But finally, the best gift—the one that truly gives back: time taken out of my busy schedule to visit assisted living facilities with my two freshly-washed Yorkshire terriers, sporting tiny Santa caps. Those wee, furry elves got lots of pats and attention as smiles spread across wrinkled, now happier, faces. So often it's the simple things that count the most.